RUNNER'S WORLD

TRAINING DIARY

By the Editors of *Runner's World* Magazine

BICENTENNIAL
1807
WILEY
2007
BICENTENNIAL

John Wiley & Sons, Inc.

This Book's Writer

PERSONAL INFORMATION

Name _____

Address _____

Phone (home) _____ (other) _____

Height _____ Weight _____ Birthdate _____

RUNNING HISTORY

Began running (year) _____ (age) _____

First run (how long?) _____ (where?) _____ (when?) _____

First race (how long?) _____ (where?) _____ (when?) _____

Briefly describe the high and low points of your running career to date:

Why a Diary?

My diary taught me almost all I know of running. It showed me how to run, how to think about what I'd run and how to write about running.

Of course, I didn't suspect any of this would happen in November 1959 when I made my first entry in a little black book given to me by the Libertyville Lumber Company. I only intended to note what I ran each day.

The numbers didn't mean much at first. Single days rarely do, either in running or reporting on it. The way the days add up is what counts, both on the road and on paper. It took months for mine to add up enough for patterns to emerge. But when they did, they gave me a new game to play which was as exciting as the running itself.

I saw certain types and amounts of running gave certain results, good and bad. I learned more about training and racing from rereading my own scribbled history than from any of the books by the giants of coaching in the 1950s and '60s. Stampfl, Cerutty and Lydiard gave their theories. The diaries listed my trial-and-error practice.

Far more days went to trying and erring than to real learning. But in between the insights, I fixed the habits of keeping records and, later, writing down observations each day. This took only a few minutes, but it added up to far more than I ever thought it could.

The running diaries have long since evolved into something else. They are now a writing journal storing the raw materials of my trade. Yet I have my priorities. At the top of each day's writing is a line telling where, how much and how well I ran. Everything I do as a runner ends there, while everything I do as a writer only starts there.

Lined up now on a full two shelves of my office are fat notebooks labeled "1986," "1985" and so on, all the way back to "1959." I'm prouder of them than of anything I've published, because they are the evidence of where I've been. They are memorials to myself.

I don't want everyone to start writing with the idea of becoming a paid author. There's too much competition in the field already. But I urge everyone who runs to keep a diary. At the least, you'll give yourself a place to brag and complain without boring anyone else. At best, you'll teach yourself how to run better and maybe even how to live better.

We give you a skeleton of a diary. You have to provide the effort to flesh it out and give it life. Run first, and then write what you did. Don't worry about style, since probably no one but you will ever read it. Just make this a daily note to yourself.

The book has two types of daily diaries. The first is for runners in a hurry. All you need to do is mark your mileage on a calendar and keep a running total for each week. One page holds a full year's running.

The second type carries more detail. Each page shows a week. Each day gives 10 factors to report. This diary also has enough space for a year of running.

Since it's your book, you can write in or ignore any of the spaces. Most items don't need explaining here. They deal with when, where and how much. Weather directly affects a run, so data on temperature, humidity, precipitation and cloud cover might be noted. Body weight and resting pulse rate are sensitive indicators of fitness that can be read easily.

The grade shows how satisfying the run was. I rate mine as if they were tests in school: A = excellent; B = good; C = fair; D = poor; F = awful. You can set your own qualifying standards. Mine are based on how well or poorly I hit distance target, and on how much or how little I hurt.

A sample entry: (see next page)

Add any extra comments at the bottom of a week's page. More details on a race might go there, for instance, as well as in other tables we provide as aids in record-keeping.

Several charts on such matters as pacing, heat, cold and weight are included for quick reference. However, this remains largely a blank book for you to write yourself—the raw material with which to begin your own memorial to yourself.

—Joe Henderson

WEEK OF _January 7-13_
GOALS FOR WEEK _Start 8-week buildup_
for marathon March — 50 miles

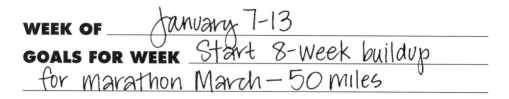

No one talks or writes so enthusiastically as when he is telling someone else what is bad for him. But convincing him of the errors of his ways is only half the job. The other half is outlining a corrective program.

SUNDAY 7th

Tired from yesterday's long run.

Pace __8:18__ Weather __32° clear__ Distance __5__ Week total __5__

MONDAY 8th

Still low on energy.

Pace __7:57__ Weather __35° clear__ Distance __6__ Week total __11__

TUESDAY 9th

Sub-8:00 despite snow!!

Pace __7:50__ Weather __30° Snow__ Distance __8__ Week total __19__

WEDNESDAY 10th

Felt _great_ again!!

Pace __7:48__ Weather __15°__ Distance __5__ Week total __24__

THURSDAY 11th

Too cold and windy

Pace __8:17__ Weather __20° Wind__ Distance __8__ Week total __32__

FRIDAY 12th

Easy day.

Pace __7:49__ Weather __28°__ Distance __4__ Week total __36__

SATURDAY 13th

Longest run in 3 months.

Pace __8:32__ Weather __30°__ Distance __14__ Week total __(50)__

SUMMARY

No real problem with a 50-mile week. Move to 55.

Week's total __50 mi__ Longest run __14 mi__ Shortest run __4 mi__

Average run __7.1__ Month's total __81__ Year's total __81__

Daily Weight		
	Wed	145
Sun 145	Thurs	144
Mon 146	Fri	144
Tues 145	Sat	143

Morning Pulse		
	Wed	55
Sun 56	Thurs	56
Mon 54	Fri	54
Tues 54	Sat	54

Quick Diary

	January	February	March	April	May	June
1						
2						
3						
4						
5						
6						
7						
8						
9						
10						
11						
12						
13						
14						
15						
16						
17						
18						
19						
20						
21						
22						
23						
24						
25						
26						
27						
28						
29						
30						
31						
TOTAL						

A full year's training mileage at a glance

Year _____

	July	August	September	October	November	December
1						
2						
3						
4						
5						
6						
7						
8						
9						
10						
11						
12						
13						
14						
15						
16						
17						
18						
19						
20						
21						
22						
23						
24						
25						
26						
27						
28						
29						
30						
31						
TOTAL						

Record the day's mileage and a running total for the week—for example: "1–6 mi./26"

Full-Year Training Graph

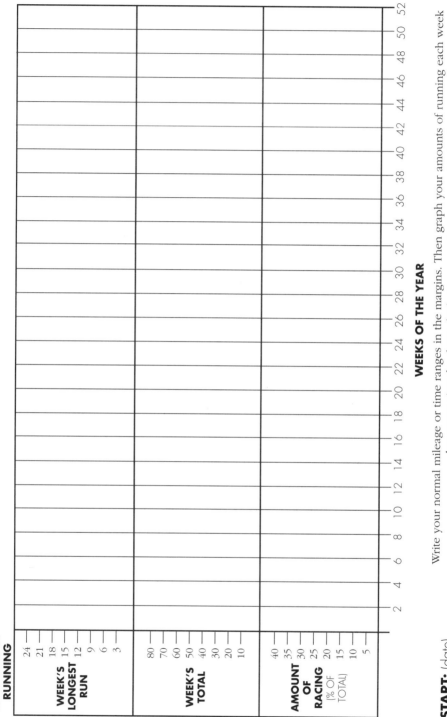

AMOUNTS OF RUNNING

WEEK'S LONGEST RUN
24 21 18 15 12 9 6 3

WEEK'S TOTAL
80 70 60 50 40 30 20 10

AMOUNT OF RACING (% OF TOTAL)
40 35 30 25 20 15 10 5

WEEKS OF THE YEAR
2 4 6 8 10 12 14 16 18 20 22 24 26 28 30 32 34 36 38 40 42 44 46 48 50 52

Write your normal mileage or time ranges in the margins. Then graph your amounts of running each week by connecting the dots which correspond to your weekly totals.

START: (date) _____

NOTES

WEEK OF _____

GOALS FOR WEEK _____

No one talks or writes so enthusiastically as when he is telling someone else what is bad for him. But convincing him of the errors of his ways is only half the job. The other half is outlining a corrective program.

SUNDAY

Pace _____ Weather _____ Distance _____ Week total _____

MONDAY

Pace _____ Weather _____ Distance _____ Week total _____

TUESDAY

Pace _____ Weather _____ Distance _____ Week total _____

WEDNESDAY

Pace _____ Weather _____ Distance _____ Week total _____

THURSDAY

Pace _____ Weather _____ Distance _____ Week total _____

FRIDAY

Pace _____ Weather _____ Distance _____ Week total _____

SATURDAY

Pace _____ Weather _____ Distance _____ Week total _____

SUMMARY

Week's total _____ Longest run _____ Shortest run _____

Average run _____ Month's total _____ Year's total _____

Daily Weight

	Wed _____
Sun _____	Thurs _____
Mon _____	Fri _____
Tues _____	Sat _____

Morning Pulse

	Wed _____
Sun _____	Thurs _____
Mon _____	Fri _____
Tues _____	Sat _____

WEEK OF _____

GOALS FOR WEEK _____

_____

The Big Lie on the physical side of running is, "If it is going to help you, it has to hurt." The Lie is spread by people who confuse pain with purpose. The fact is, pain in running serves no purpose except to prevent you from inflicting more pain on yourself. It draws boundaries which you cross only at great risk.

SUNDAY

Pace _____ Weather _____ Distance _____ Week total _____

MONDAY

Pace _____ Weather _____ Distance _____ Week total _____

TUESDAY

Pace _____ Weather _____ Distance _____ Week total _____

WEDNESDAY

Pace _____ Weather _____ Distance _____ Week total _____

THURSDAY

Pace _____ Weather _____ Distance _____ Week total _____

FRIDAY

Pace _____ Weather _____ Distance _____ Week total _____

SATURDAY

Pace _____ Weather _____ Distance _____ Week total _____

SUMMARY

Week's total _____ Longest run _____ Shortest run _____

Average run _____ Month's total _____ Year's total _____

Daily Weight   Wed _____

Sun _____   Thurs _____

Mon _____   Fri _____

Tues _____   Sat _____

Morning Pulse   Wed _____

Sun _____   Thurs _____

Mon _____   Fri _____

Tues _____   Sat _____

WEEK OF _____

GOALS FOR WEEK _____

_____

There is a Big Lie on the psychological side as well. "Running is, by its nature, a lonely and boring activity." This fallacy lives in the minds of people who confuse aloneness with loneliness and unstructured activity with boredom. They aren't the same. In fact, in many ways they are direct opposites.

SUNDAY

Pace _____ Weather _____ Distance _____ Week total _____

MONDAY

Pace _____ Weather _____ Distance _____ Week total _____

TUESDAY

Pace _____ Weather _____ Distance _____ Week total _____

WEDNESDAY

Pace _____ Weather _____ Distance _____ Week total _____

THURSDAY

Pace _____ Weather _____ Distance _____ Week total _____

FRIDAY

Pace _____ Weather _____ Distance _____ Week total _____

SATURDAY

Pace _____ Weather _____ Distance _____ Week total _____

SUMMARY

Week's total _____ Longest run _____ Shortest run _____

Average run _____ Month's total _____ Year's total _____

Daily Weight

		Wed	_____
Sun	_____	Thurs	_____
Mon	_____	Fri	_____
Tues	_____	Sat	_____

Morning Pulse

		Wed	_____
Sun	_____	Thurs	_____
Mon	_____	Fri	_____
Tues	_____	Sat	_____

WEEK OF _____

GOALS FOR WEEK _____

_____

There is no shortage of talk in this turned-on, turned-in world. But as the world grows busier and noisier, we let shrink that essential time each day to be alone to fantasize, to reflect, to clear away cluttering thoughts, to plan.

SUNDAY

Pace _____ Weather _____ Distance _____ Week total _____

MONDAY

Pace _____ Weather _____ Distance _____ Week total _____

TUESDAY

Pace _____ Weather _____ Distance _____ Week total _____

WEDNESDAY

Pace _____ Weather _____ Distance _____ Week total _____

THURSDAY

Pace _____ Weather _____ Distance _____ Week total _____

FRIDAY

Pace _____ Weather _____ Distance _____ Week total _____

SATURDAY

Pace _____ Weather _____ Distance _____ Week total _____

SUMMARY

Week's total _____ Longest run _____ Shortest run _____

Average run _____ Month's total _____ Year's total _____

Daily Weight   Wed _____

Sun _____   Thurs _____

Mon _____   Fri _____

Tues _____   Sat _____

Morning Pulse   Wed _____

Sun _____   Thurs _____

Mon _____   Fri _____

Tues _____   Sat _____

WEEK OF _____

GOALS FOR WEEK _____

_____

You run to no one's beat but your own. No one else is making you run. No one else cares whether you do it or not. The responsibility for running is yours entirely, and the same can be said for the rewards in doing it. They are all yours too.

SUNDAY

Pace _____ Weather _____ Distance _____ Week total _____

MONDAY

Pace _____ Weather _____ Distance _____ Week total _____

TUESDAY

Pace _____ Weather _____ Distance _____ Week total _____

WEDNESDAY

Pace _____ Weather _____ Distance _____ Week total _____

THURSDAY

Pace _____ Weather _____ Distance _____ Week total _____

FRIDAY

Pace _____ Weather _____ Distance _____ Week total _____

SATURDAY

Pace _____ Weather _____ Distance _____ Week total _____

SUMMARY

Week's total _____ Longest run _____ Shortest run _____

Average run _____ Month's total _____ Year's total _____

Daily Weight   Wed _____

Sun _____   Thurs _____

Mon _____   Fri _____

Tues _____   Sat _____

Morning Pulse   Wed _____

Sun _____   Thurs _____

Mon _____   Fri _____

Tues _____   Sat _____

WEEK OF _____

GOALS FOR WEEK _____

_____

The first 20 or 30 minutes of a run make a person fit. Most of the physical benefits can be had in that short time, and the returns diminish quickly from then on.

SUNDAY

Pace _____ Weather _____ Distance _____ Week total _____

MONDAY

Pace _____ Weather _____ Distance _____ Week total _____

TUESDAY

Pace _____ Weather _____ Distance _____ Week total _____

WEDNESDAY

Pace _____ Weather _____ Distance _____ Week total _____

THURSDAY

Pace _____ Weather _____ Distance _____ Week total _____

FRIDAY

Pace _____ Weather _____ Distance _____ Week total _____

SATURDAY

Pace _____ Weather _____ Distance _____ Week total _____

SUMMARY

Week's total _____ Longest run _____ Shortest run _____

Average run _____ Month's total _____ Year's total _____

Daily Weight	Wed _____	**Morning Pulse**	Wed _____
Sun _____	Thurs _____	Sun _____	Thurs _____
Mon _____	Fri _____	Mon _____	Fri _____
Tues _____	Sat _____	Tues _____	Sat _____

WEEK OF _____

GOALS FOR WEEK _____

_____

I t is the second 20 or 30 minutes that make running worth doing. That's when it starts to feel good and to make you glad you did the first part. The extra 20 or 30 minutes make you want to come back for more.

SUNDAY

Pace _____ Weather _____ Distance _____ Week total _____

MONDAY

Pace _____ Weather _____ Distance _____ Week total _____

TUESDAY

Pace _____ Weather _____ Distance _____ Week total _____

WEDNESDAY

Pace _____ Weather _____ Distance _____ Week total _____

THURSDAY

Pace _____ Weather _____ Distance _____ Week total _____

FRIDAY

Pace _____ Weather _____ Distance _____ Week total _____

SATURDAY

Pace _____ Weather _____ Distance _____ Week total _____

SUMMARY

Week's total _____ Longest run _____ Shortest run _____

Average run _____ Month's total _____ Year's total _____

Daily Weight   Wed _____

Sun _____   Thurs _____

Mon _____   Fri _____

Tues _____   Sat _____

Morning Pulse   Wed _____

Sun _____   Thurs _____

Mon _____   Fri _____

Tues _____   Sat _____

WEEK OF _____

GOALS FOR WEEK _____

_____

J ust as runners start to run alone because they must, and continue because they learn to like themselves, they sometimes come together for practical reasons and keep coming back for social ones.

SUNDAY

Pace _____ Weather _____ Distance _____ Week total _____

MONDAY

Pace _____ Weather _____ Distance _____ Week total _____

TUESDAY

Pace _____ Weather _____ Distance _____ Week total _____

WEDNESDAY

Pace _____ Weather _____ Distance _____ Week total _____

THURSDAY

Pace _____ Weather _____ Distance _____ Week total _____

FRIDAY

Pace _____ Weather _____ Distance _____ Week total _____

SATURDAY

Pace _____ Weather _____ Distance _____ Week total _____

SUMMARY

Week's total _____ Longest run _____ Shortest run _____

Average run _____ Month's total _____ Year's total _____

Daily Weight

Wed _____

Sun _____   Thurs _____

Mon _____   Fri _____

Tues _____   Sat _____

Morning Pulse

Wed _____

Sun _____   Thurs _____

Mon _____   Fri _____

Tues _____   Sat _____

WEEK OF _____

GOALS FOR WEEK _____

_____

The deeper you plunge into fun-running, the less important the physical returns are to you. They have value, of course, but are something like the gas mileage of your car. They are the by-product of having an efficient engine which is kept in good tune, but they have little to do with how much you enjoy your travels.

SUNDAY

Pace _____ Weather _____ Distance _____ Week total _____

MONDAY

Pace _____ Weather _____ Distance _____ Week total _____

TUESDAY

Pace _____ Weather _____ Distance _____ Week total _____

WEDNESDAY

Pace _____ Weather _____ Distance _____ Week total _____

THURSDAY

Pace _____ Weather _____ Distance _____ Week total _____

FRIDAY

Pace _____ Weather _____ Distance _____ Week total _____

SATURDAY

Pace _____ Weather _____ Distance _____ Week total _____

SUMMARY

Week's total _____ Longest run _____ Shortest run _____

Average run _____ Month's total _____ Year's total _____

Daily Weight
		Wed	_____
Sun	_____	Thurs	_____
Mon	_____	Fri	_____
Tues	_____	Sat	_____

Morning Pulse
		Wed	_____
Sun	_____	Thurs	_____
Mon	_____	Fri	_____
Tues	_____	Sat	_____

Runners share a secret. We know we may look and act a little weird by the standards of the sitdown world, but we know too that our running is setting free the thoughts, words and sensations which stagnate in non-movers.

SUNDAY

Pace _____ Weather _____ Distance _____ Week total _____

MONDAY

Pace _____ Weather _____ Distance _____ Week total _____

TUESDAY

Pace _____ Weather _____ Distance _____ Week total _____

WEDNESDAY

Pace _____ Weather _____ Distance _____ Week total _____

THURSDAY

Pace _____ Weather _____ Distance _____ Week total _____

FRIDAY

Pace _____ Weather _____ Distance _____ Week total _____

SATURDAY

Pace _____ Weather _____ Distance _____ Week total _____

SUMMARY

Week's total _____ Longest run _____ Shortest run _____

Average run _____ Month's total _____ Year's total _____

Daily Weight

Wed _____

Sun _____   Thurs _____

Mon _____   Fri _____

Tues _____   Sat _____

Morning Pulse

Wed _____

Sun _____   Thurs _____

Mon _____   Fri _____

Tues _____   Sat _____

GOALS FOR WEEK _____

_____

You run best when you cooperate with yourself and your environment, coaxing out the benefits. You race best when you work against your natural instincts to slow down and avoid pain. In racing, you make a direct challenge to distance, time, terrain and other racers.

SUNDAY

Pace _____ Weather _____ Distance _____ Week total _____

MONDAY

Pace _____ Weather _____ Distance _____ Week total _____

TUESDAY

Pace _____ Weather _____ Distance _____ Week total _____

WEDNESDAY

Pace _____ Weather _____ Distance _____ Week total _____

THURSDAY

Pace _____ Weather _____ Distance _____ Week total _____

FRIDAY

Pace _____ Weather _____ Distance _____ Week total _____

SATURDAY

Pace _____ Weather _____ Distance _____ Week total _____

SUMMARY

Week's total _____ Longest run _____ Shortest run _____

Average run _____ Month's total _____ Year's total _____

Daily Weight

		Wed	_____
Sun	_____	Thurs	_____
Mon	_____	Fri	_____
Tues	_____	Sat	_____

Morning Pulse

		Wed	_____
Sun	_____	Thurs	_____
Mon	_____	Fri	_____
Tues	_____	Sat	_____

WEEK OF _____

GOALS FOR WEEK _____

_____

Realize it's normal to feel anxious and uncertain as you approach a race, because your nerves are getting you ready for hard work which you couldn't handle if you were calm. And accept the temporary pain that goes with racing effort, because overcoming pain makes racing worthwhile.

SUNDAY

Pace _____ Weather _____ Distance _____ Week total _____

MONDAY

Pace _____ Weather _____ Distance _____ Week total _____

TUESDAY

Pace _____ Weather _____ Distance _____ Week total _____

WEDNESDAY

Pace _____ Weather _____ Distance _____ Week total _____

THURSDAY

Pace _____ Weather _____ Distance _____ Week total _____

FRIDAY

Pace _____ Weather _____ Distance _____ Week total _____

SATURDAY

Pace _____ Weather _____ Distance _____ Week total _____

SUMMARY

Week's total _____ Longest run _____ Shortest run _____

Average run _____ Month's total _____ Year's total _____

Daily Weight   Wed _____

Sun _____   Thurs _____

Mon _____   Fri _____

Tues _____   Sat _____

Morning Pulse   Wed _____

Sun _____   Thurs _____

Mon _____   Fri _____

Tues _____   Sat _____

WEEK OF _____

GOALS FOR WEEK _____

_____

As a runner, you are what you *run*, not what you eat. Dietary practices may smooth or block the path of running, but they don't provide any shortcuts.

SUNDAY

Pace _____ Weather _____ Distance _____ Week total _____

MONDAY

Pace _____ Weather _____ Distance _____ Week total _____

TUESDAY

Pace _____ Weather _____ Distance _____ Week total _____

WEDNESDAY

Pace _____ Weather _____ Distance _____ Week total _____

THURSDAY

Pace _____ Weather _____ Distance _____ Week total _____

FRIDAY

Pace _____ Weather _____ Distance _____ Week total _____

SATURDAY

Pace _____ Weather _____ Distance _____ Week total _____

SUMMARY

Week's total _____ Longest run _____ Shortest run _____

Average run _____ Month's total _____ Year's total _____

Daily Weight

Wed _____

Sun _____   Thurs _____

Mon _____   Fri _____

Tues _____   Sat _____

Morning Pulse

Wed _____

Sun _____   Thurs _____

Mon _____   Fri _____

Tues _____   Sat _____

WEEK OF _____

GOALS FOR WEEK _____

Without question, dietary quantity has the most direct influence on running. How much you eat determines how much you weigh and your weight is what you carry with you. They less baggage you carry, the easier you run.

SUNDAY

Pace _____ Weather _____ Distance _____ Week total _____

MONDAY

Pace _____ Weather _____ Distance _____ Week total _____

TUESDAY

Pace _____ Weather _____ Distance _____ Week total _____

WEDNESDAY

Pace _____ Weather _____ Distance _____ Week total _____

THURSDAY

Pace _____ Weather _____ Distance _____ Week total _____

FRIDAY

Pace _____ Weather _____ Distance _____ Week total _____

SATURDAY

Pace _____ Weather _____ Distance _____ Week total _____

SUMMARY

Week's total _____ Longest run _____ Shortest run _____

Average run _____ Month's total _____ Year's total _____

Daily Weight

		Wed	_____
Sun	_____	Thurs	_____
Mon	_____	Fri	_____
Tues	_____	Sat	_____

Morning Pulse

		Wed	_____
Sun	_____	Thurs	_____
Mon	_____	Fri	_____
Tues	_____	Sat	_____

WEEK OF _____

GOALS FOR WEEK _____

_____

Serious running ailments need not happen. They do happen, of course, but they can be prevented if you are flexible in every sense of the word. Flexibility of the muscles is important, yes, but flexibility of the *mind* is much more so. Bend your running schedule to fit your feelings, not the other way around.

SUNDAY

Pace _____ Weather _____ Distance _____ Week total _____

MONDAY

Pace _____ Weather _____ Distance _____ Week total _____

TUESDAY

Pace _____ Weather _____ Distance _____ Week total _____

WEDNESDAY

Pace _____ Weather _____ Distance _____ Week total _____

THURSDAY

Pace _____ Weather _____ Distance _____ Week total _____

FRIDAY

Pace _____ Weather _____ Distance _____ Week total _____

SATURDAY

Pace _____ Weather _____ Distance _____ Week total _____

SUMMARY

Week's total _____ Longest run _____ Shortest run _____

Average run _____ Month's total _____ Year's total _____

Daily Weight

Wed _____

Sun _____   Thurs _____

Mon _____   Fri _____

Tues _____   Sat _____

Morning Pulse

Wed _____

Sun _____   Thurs _____

Mon _____   Fri _____

Tues _____   Sat _____

GOALS FOR WEEK _____

_____

The general rule for running after an injury or illness has occurred is this: If the symptoms decrease or disappear as you go, keep going. You probably aren't doing yourself further harm. But if the symptoms grow as you go, stop before you hurt yourself any more.

SUNDAY

Pace_____ Weather _____ Distance _____ Week total_____

MONDAY

Pace_____ Weather _____ Distance _____ Week total_____

TUESDAY

Pace_____ Weather _____ Distance _____ Week total_____

WEDNESDAY

Pace_____ Weather _____ Distance _____ Week total_____

THURSDAY

Pace_____ Weather_____ Distance_____ Week total_____

FRIDAY

Pace_____ Weather_____ Distance_____ Week total_____

SATURDAY

Pace_____ Weather_____ Distance_____ Week total_____

SUMMARY

Week's total _____ Longest run _____ Shortest run _____

Average run _____ Month's total _____ Year's total _____

Daily Weight

	Wed _____
Sun _____	Thurs _____
Mon _____	Fri _____
Tues _____	Sat _____

Morning Pulse

	Wed _____
Sun _____	Thurs _____
Mon _____	Fri _____
Tues _____	Sat _____

WEEK OF _____

GOALS FOR WEEK _____

_____

The marathon is the ultimate endurance test. Oh sure, people sometimes go longer than that. But 26 miles 385 yards is where racing ends and where ludicrous extremes begin.

SUNDAY

Pace _____ Weather _____ Distance _____ Week total _____

MONDAY

Pace _____ Weather _____ Distance _____ Week total _____

TUESDAY

Pace _____ Weather _____ Distance _____ Week total _____

WEDNESDAY

Pace _____ Weather _____ Distance _____ Week total _____

THURSDAY

Pace _____ Weather _____ Distance _____ Week total _____

FRIDAY

Pace _____ Weather _____ Distance _____ Week total _____

SATURDAY

Pace _____ Weather _____ Distance _____ Week total _____

SUMMARY

Week's total _____ Longest run _____ Shortest run _____

Average run _____ Month's total _____ Year's total _____

Daily Weight

Wed _____

Sun _____ Thurs _____

Mon _____ Fri _____

Tues _____ Sat _____

Morning Pulse

Wed _____

Sun _____ Thurs _____

Mon _____ Fri _____

Tues _____ Sat _____

WEEK OF _____

GOALS FOR WEEK _____

_____

The mile is the perfect test of prolonged speed. It is long enough to demand the intelligent pacing and tactics of a distance runner, but short enough that it requires the explosiveness of a sprinter.

SUNDAY

Pace _____ Weather _____ Distance _____ Week total _____

MONDAY

Pace _____ Weather _____ Distance _____ Week total _____

TUESDAY

Pace _____ Weather _____ Distance _____ Week total _____

WEDNESDAY

Pace _____ Weather _____ Distance _____ Week total _____

THURSDAY

Pace _____ Weather _____ Distance _____ Week total _____

FRIDAY

Pace _____ Weather _____ Distance _____ Week total _____

SATURDAY

Pace _____ Weather _____ Distance _____ Week total _____

SUMMARY

Week's total _____ Longest run _____ Shortest run _____

Average run _____ Month's total _____ Year's total _____

Daily Weight

		Wed	_____
Sun	_____	Thurs	_____
Mon	_____	Fri	_____
Tues	_____	Sat	_____

Morning Pulse

		Wed	_____
Sun	_____	Thurs	_____
Mon	_____	Fri	_____
Tues	_____	Sat	_____

GOALS FOR WEEK _____

_____

emember the rule: endurance first, speed later. You pick up much of your
speed not by training fast but by increasing your staying power. You can't do
much more than sharpen up the speed you were born with, but you can train yourself not to poop out so soon when you're going fast if you practice at distances a lot
longer than a mile.

SUNDAY

Pace _____ Weather _____ Distance _____ Week total _____

MONDAY

Pace _____ Weather _____ Distance _____ Week total _____

TUESDAY

Pace _____ Weather _____ Distance _____ Week total _____

WEDNESDAY

Pace _____ Weather _____ Distance _____ Week total _____

THURSDAY

Pace _____ Weather _____ Distance _____ Week total _____

FRIDAY

Pace _____ Weather _____ Distance _____ Week total _____

SATURDAY

Pace _____ Weather _____ Distance _____ Week total _____

SUMMARY

Week's total _____ Longest run _____ Shortest run _____

Average run _____ Month's total _____ Year's total _____

Daily Weight

	Wed _____
Sun _____	Thurs _____
Mon _____	Fri _____
Tues _____	Sat _____

Morning Pulse

	Wed _____
Sun _____	Thurs _____
Mon _____	Fri _____
Tues _____	Sat _____

WEEK OF _____

GOALS FOR WEEK _____

_____

Running authority Hal Higdon has written, "Perhaps the most cogent comment I can make on speed training is that the top runners use it too much and the bottom runners use it too little. . . . My advice would be that the speed runners do less and the slow runners do more, and maybe we'll all meet in the middle."

SUNDAY

Pace _____ Weather _____ Distance _____ Week total _____

MONDAY

Pace _____ Weather _____ Distance _____ Week total _____

TUESDAY

Pace _____ Weather _____ Distance _____ Week total _____

WEDNESDAY

Pace _____ Weather _____ Distance _____ Week total _____

THURSDAY

Pace _____ Weather _____ Distance _____ Week total _____

FRIDAY

Pace _____ Weather _____ Distance _____ Week total _____

SATURDAY

Pace _____ Weather _____ Distance _____ Week total _____

SUMMARY

Week's total _____ Longest run _____ Shortest run _____

Average run _____ Month's total _____ Year's total _____

Daily Weight   Wed _____

Sun _____   Thurs _____

Mon _____   Fri _____

Tues _____   Sat _____

Morning Pulse   Wed _____

Sun _____   Thurs _____

Mon _____   Fri _____

Tues _____   Sat _____

WEEK OF _____

GOALS FOR WEEK _____

_____

If you don't feel at all hungry, just don't eat. As Coach Arthur Lydiard has said, he's seen thousands of races and he's never seen anyone collapse from malnutrition yet. You aren't going to faint if you haven't eaten anything since the night before. But you might cramp up or throw up if you force something down.

SUNDAY

Pace _____ Weather _____ Distance _____ Week total _____

MONDAY

Pace _____ Weather _____ Distance _____ Week total _____

TUESDAY

Pace _____ Weather _____ Distance _____ Week total _____

WEDNESDAY

Pace _____ Weather _____ Distance _____ Week total _____

THURSDAY

Pace _____ Weather _____ Distance _____ Week total _____

FRIDAY

Pace _____ Weather _____ Distance _____ Week total _____

SATURDAY

Pace _____ Weather _____ Distance _____ Week total _____

SUMMARY

Week's total _____ Longest run _____ Shortest run _____

Average run _____ Month's total _____ Year's total _____

Daily Weight

Wed _____

Sun _____ Thurs _____

Mon _____ Fri _____

Tues _____ Sat _____

Morning Pulse

Wed _____

Sun _____ Thurs _____

Mon _____ Fri _____

Tues _____ Sat _____

WEEK OF _____

GOALS FOR WEEK _____

_____

The final stage of recovery is psychological. Experienced runners say, "You aren't ready to think about another race until you've forgotten how bad the last one felt." This may take weeks for a miler, months for a marathoner.

SUNDAY

Pace _____ Weather _____ Distance _____ Week total _____

MONDAY

Pace _____ Weather _____ Distance _____ Week total _____

TUESDAY

Pace _____ Weather _____ Distance _____ Week total _____

WEDNESDAY

Pace _____ Weather _____ Distance _____ Week total _____

THURSDAY

Pace _____ Weather _____ Distance _____ Week total _____

FRIDAY

Pace _____ Weather _____ Distance _____ Week total _____

SATURDAY

Pace _____ Weather _____ Distance _____ Week total _____

SUMMARY

Week's total _____ Longest run _____ Shortest run _____

Average run _____ Month's total _____ Year's total _____

Daily Weight

	Wed _____
Sun _____	Thurs _____
Mon _____	Fri _____
Tues _____	Sat _____

Morning Pulse

	Wed _____
Sun _____	Thurs _____
Mon _____	Fri _____
Tues _____	Sat _____

WEEK OF _____

GOALS FOR WEEK _____

_____

Running does no good if it doesn't last. After a few months away from it, even a world record holder or Olympic champion is no more of a runner than the next slob on the street.

SUNDAY

Pace _____ Weather _____ Distance _____ Week total _____

MONDAY

Pace _____ Weather _____ Distance _____ Week total _____

TUESDAY

Pace _____ Weather _____ Distance _____ Week total _____

WEDNESDAY

Pace _____ Weather _____ Distance _____ Week total _____

THURSDAY

Pace _____ Weather _____ Distance _____ Week total _____

FRIDAY

Pace _____ Weather _____ Distance _____ Week total _____

SATURDAY

Pace _____ Weather _____ Distance _____ Week total _____

SUMMARY

Week's total _____ Longest run _____ Shortest run _____

Average run_____ Month's total _____ Year's total_____

Daily Weight   Wed _____

Sun _____   Thurs _____

Mon _____   Fri _____

Tues _____   Sat _____

Morning Pulse   Wed _____

Sun _____   Thurs _____

Mon _____   Fri _____

Tues _____   Sat _____

WEEK OF _____

GOALS FOR WEEK _____

_____

Too much physical stress, too much psychological tension, too many goals unmet are the reasons why runners become ex-runners.

SUNDAY

Pace _____ Weather _____ Distance _____ Week total _____

MONDAY

Pace _____ Weather _____ Distance _____ Week total _____

TUESDAY

Pace _____ Weather _____ Distance _____ Week total _____

WEDNESDAY

Pace _____ Weather _____ Distance _____ Week total _____

THURSDAY

Pace_____ Weather _____ Distance _____ Week total _____

FRIDAY

Pace_____ Weather _____ Distance _____ Week total _____

SATURDAY

Pace_____ Weather _____ Distance _____ Week total _____

SUMMARY

Week's total _____ Longest run _____ Shortest run _____

Average run_____ Month's total _____ Year's total_____

Daily Weight

	Wed _____
Sun _____	Thurs _____
Mon _____	Fri _____
Tues _____	Sat _____

Morning Pulse

	Wed _____
Sun _____	Thurs _____
Mon _____	Fri _____
Tues _____	Sat _____

WEEK OF _____

GOALS FOR WEEK _____

_____

The secret to good running is simply to keep going. And the way to keep at it is to keep the distances and paces modest, and to keep healthy and happy.

SUNDAY

Pace _____ Weather _____ Distance _____ Week total _____

MONDAY

Pace _____ Weather _____ Distance _____ Week total _____

TUESDAY

Pace _____ Weather _____ Distance _____ Week total _____

WEDNESDAY

Pace _____ Weather _____ Distance _____ Week total _____

THURSDAY

Pace _____ Weather _____ Distance _____ Week total _____

FRIDAY

Pace _____ Weather _____ Distance _____ Week total _____

SATURDAY

Pace _____ Weather _____ Distance _____ Week total _____

SUMMARY

Week's total _____ Longest run _____ Shortest run _____

Average run _____ Month's total _____ Year's total _____

Daily Weight

	Wed _____
Sun _____	Thurs _____
Mon _____	Fri _____
Tues _____	Sat _____

Morning Pulse

	Wed _____
Sun _____	Thurs _____
Mon _____	Fri _____
Tues _____	Sat _____

WEEK OF _____

GOALS FOR WEEK _____

D on't wait. Run while you feel like it, in the way you think you should. Do it on the track or on the street. Sprint or jog or combine the two. Race the clock, or race an imaginary opponent, or try to finish a distance you've set for yourself. Do whatever you want, but do it.

SUNDAY

Pace _____ Weather _____ Distance _____ Week total _____

MONDAY

Pace _____ Weather _____ Distance _____ Week total _____

TUESDAY

Pace _____ Weather _____ Distance _____ Week total _____

WEDNESDAY

Pace _____ Weather _____ Distance _____ Week total _____

THURSDAY

Pace _____ Weather _____ Distance _____ Week total _____

FRIDAY

Pace _____ Weather _____ Distance _____ Week total _____

SATURDAY

Pace _____ Weather _____ Distance _____ Week total _____

SUMMARY

Week's total _____ Longest run _____ Shortest run _____

Average run_____ Month's total _____ Year's total_____

Daily Weight   Wed _____

Sun _____   Thurs _____

Mon _____   Fri _____

Tues _____   Sat _____

Morning Pulse   Wed _____

Sun _____   Thurs _____

Mon _____   Fri _____

Tues _____   Sat _____

Pain can be a good teacher. It can force lessons on you which you never would have noticed had the run been easy and pleasant. Later, you'll make adjustments based on these lessons, and you'll know exactly why you're making them, since avoidance of pain is one of man's basic drives.

SUNDAY

Pace _____ Weather _____ Distance _____ Week total _____

MONDAY

Pace _____ Weather _____ Distance _____ Week total _____

TUESDAY

Pace _____ Weather _____ Distance _____ Week total _____

WEDNESDAY

Pace _____ Weather _____ Distance _____ Week total _____

THURSDAY

Pace _____ Weather _____ Distance _____ Week total _____

FRIDAY

Pace _____ Weather _____ Distance _____ Week total _____

SATURDAY

Pace _____ Weather _____ Distance _____ Week total _____

SUMMARY

Week's total _____ Longest run _____ Shortest run _____

Average run _____ Month's total _____ Year's total _____

Daily Weight

	Wed _____
Sun _____	Thurs _____
Mon _____	Fri _____
Tues _____	Sat _____

Morning Pulse

	Wed _____
Sun _____	Thurs _____
Mon _____	Fri _____
Tues _____	Sat _____

WEEK OF _____

GOALS FOR WEEK _____

Restraint, holding back a little bit, stopping short. These are key concepts in running. Distance running is a process of rationing out effort, of intentionally running at something less than your best effort so you are able to keep going for a longer time.

SUNDAY

Pace _____ Weather _____ Distance _____ Week total _____

MONDAY

Pace _____ Weather _____ Distance _____ Week total _____

TUESDAY

Pace _____ Weather _____ Distance _____ Week total _____

WEDNESDAY

Pace _____ Weather _____ Distance _____ Week total _____

THURSDAY

Pace _____ Weather _____ Distance _____ Week total _____

FRIDAY

Pace _____ Weather _____ Distance _____ Week total _____

SATURDAY

Pace _____ Weather _____ Distance _____ Week total _____

SUMMARY

Week's total _____ Longest run _____ Shortest run _____

Average run _____ Month's total _____ Year's total _____

Daily Weight

Wed _____

Sun _____   Thurs _____

Mon _____   Fri _____

Tues _____   Sat _____

Morning Pulse

Wed _____

Sun _____   Thurs _____

Mon _____   Fri _____

Tues _____   Sat _____

WEEK OF _____

GOALS FOR WEEK _____

_____

One of the greatest accomplishments and curses of 20th century technology is that it has eliminated most self-propelled movement, making it voluntary instead of required. The strange twist in this shift is that as we are required to do less moving on foot, we need it more than ever. Our legs and hearts and heads are made to move, and decay sets in when they don't get the movement they need.

SUNDAY

Pace _____ Weather _____ Distance _____ Week total _____

MONDAY

Pace _____ Weather _____ Distance _____ Week total _____

TUESDAY

Pace _____ Weather _____ Distance _____ Week total _____

WEDNESDAY

Pace _____ Weather _____ Distance _____ Week total _____

THURSDAY

Pace _____ Weather _____ Distance _____ Week total _____

FRIDAY

Pace _____ Weather _____ Distance _____ Week total _____

SATURDAY

Pace _____ Weather _____ Distance _____ Week total _____

SUMMARY

Week's total _____ Longest run _____ Shortest run _____

Average run _____ Month's total _____ Year's total _____

Daily Weight

Wed _____

Sun _____   Thurs _____

Mon _____   Fri _____

Tues _____   Sat _____

Morning Pulse

Wed _____

Sun _____   Thurs _____

Mon _____   Fri _____

Tues _____   Sat _____

GOALS FOR WEEK _____

_____

George Young, the first American to run in four Olympic Games, said, "There is nothing hard about running the hundred miles a week I do. Almost anyone could do it. The hard part is making yourself roll out of bed in the morning and start running."

SUNDAY

Pace _____ Weather _____ Distance _____ Week total _____

MONDAY

Pace _____ Weather _____ Distance _____ Week total _____

TUESDAY

Pace _____ Weather _____ Distance _____ Week total _____

WEDNESDAY

Pace _____ Weather _____ Distance _____ Week total _____

THURSDAY

Pace _____ Weather _____ Distance _____ Week total _____

FRIDAY

Pace _____ Weather _____ Distance _____ Week total _____

SATURDAY

Pace _____ Weather _____ Distance _____ Week total _____

SUMMARY

Week's total _____ Longest run _____ Shortest run _____

Average run _____ Month's total _____ Year's total _____

Daily Weight

Wed _____

Sun _____   Thurs _____

Mon _____   Fri _____

Tues _____   Sat _____

Morning Pulse

Wed _____

Sun _____   Thurs _____

Mon _____   Fri _____

Tues _____   Sat _____

GOALS FOR WEEK _____

_____

Fitness is a step above health. Health is the mere absence of disease and injury, while fitness is the ability to perform physically. You can be healthy and not fit, but you can't be fit without first being healthy.

SUNDAY

Pace _____ Weather _____ Distance _____ Week total _____

MONDAY

Pace _____ Weather _____ Distance _____ Week total _____

TUESDAY

Pace _____ Weather _____ Distance _____ Week total _____

WEDNESDAY

Pace _____ Weather _____ Distance _____ Week total _____

THURSDAY

Pace _____ Weather _____ Distance _____ Week total _____

FRIDAY

Pace _____ Weather _____ Distance _____ Week total _____

SATURDAY

Pace _____ Weather _____ Distance _____ Week total _____

SUMMARY

Week's total _____ Longest run _____ Shortest run _____

Average run _____ Month's total _____ Year's total _____

Daily Weight

	Wed _____
Sun _____	Thurs _____
Mon _____	Fri _____
Tues _____	Sat _____

Morning Pulse

	Wed _____
Sun _____	Thurs _____
Mon _____	Fri _____
Tues _____	Sat _____

WEEK OF _____

GOALS FOR WEEK _____

_____

All runners get sore. But the old-timers of the sport say, "An injury is serious only if it keeps me from running." Rate the seriousness of an injury according to how much it limits activity.

SUNDAY

Pace _____ Weather _____ Distance _____ Week total _____

MONDAY

Pace _____ Weather _____ Distance _____ Week total _____

TUESDAY

Pace _____ Weather _____ Distance _____ Week total _____

WEDNESDAY

Pace _____ Weather _____ Distance _____ Week total _____

THURSDAY

Pace _____ Weather _____ Distance _____ Week total _____

FRIDAY

Pace _____ Weather _____ Distance _____ Week total _____

SATURDAY

Pace _____ Weather _____ Distance _____ Week total _____

SUMMARY

Week's total _____ Longest run _____ Shortest run _____

Average run _____ Month's total _____ Year's total _____

Daily Weight

		Wed	_____
Sun	_____	Thurs	_____
Mon	_____	Fri	_____
Tues	_____	Sat	_____

Morning Pulse

		Wed	_____
Sun	_____	Thurs	_____
Mon	_____	Fri	_____
Tues	_____	Sat	_____

WEEK OF _____

GOALS FOR WEEK _____

_____

Form is largely an individual matter. It is a runner's "trademark," established by heredity and solidified by habit. Changes aren't easily made, and innocent quirks should be left alone. Concentrate only on correcting form which has resulted from blurry ideas of what running "should" be.

SUNDAY

Pace _____ Weather _____ Distance _____ Week total _____

MONDAY

Pace _____ Weather _____ Distance _____ Week total _____

TUESDAY

Pace _____ Weather _____ Distance _____ Week total _____

WEDNESDAY

Pace _____ Weather _____ Distance _____ Week total _____

THURSDAY

Pace _____ Weather _____ Distance _____ Week total _____

FRIDAY

Pace _____ Weather _____ Distance _____ Week total _____

SATURDAY

Pace _____ Weather _____ Distance _____ Week total _____

SUMMARY

Week's total _____ Longest run _____ Shortest run _____

Average run _____ Month's total _____ Year's total _____

Daily Weight

Wed _____

Sun _____ Thurs _____

Mon _____ Fri _____

Tues _____ Sat _____

Morning Pulse

Wed _____

Sun _____ Thurs _____

Mon _____ Fri _____

Tues _____ Sat _____

WEEK OF _____

GOALS FOR WEEK _____

_____

Shoes are the first and most important investment a runner makes, because they are your only contact with the ground. Your health and performance rest on your feet, so protect them well. The rest of your clothing is just for warmth and decoration, so don't be as concerned about it.

SUNDAY

Pace_____ Weather _____ Distance _____ Week total_____

MONDAY

Pace_____ Weather _____ Distance _____ Week total_____

TUESDAY

Pace_____ Weather _____ Distance _____ Week total_____

WEDNESDAY

Pace_____ Weather _____ Distance _____ Week total_____

THURSDAY

Pace _____ Weather _____ Distance _____ Week total _____

FRIDAY

Pace _____ Weather _____ Distance _____ Week total _____

SATURDAY

Pace _____ Weather _____ Distance _____ Week total _____

SUMMARY

Week's total _____ Longest run _____ Shortest run _____

Average run _____ Month's total _____ Year's total _____

Daily Weight

Wed _____

Sun _____   Thurs _____

Mon _____   Fri _____

Tues _____   Sat _____

Morning Pulse

Wed _____

Sun _____   Thurs _____

Mon _____   Fri _____

Tues _____   Sat _____

WEEK OF _____

GOALS FOR WEEK _____

_____

In hot weather, dress minimally, run at the coolest times of day (usually the temperature is lowest at dawn), drink all you can stand before and after running (maybe even during the run, if it's a long one), and slow down or stop if you begin to feel dizzy or nauseated.

SUNDAY

Pace _____ Weather _____ Distance _____ Week total _____

MONDAY

Pace _____ Weather _____ Distance _____ Week total _____

TUESDAY

Pace _____ Weather _____ Distance _____ Week total _____

WEDNESDAY

Pace _____ Weather _____ Distance _____ Week total _____

THURSDAY

Pace _____ Weather _____ Distance _____ Week total _____

FRIDAY

Pace _____ Weather _____ Distance _____ Week total _____

SATURDAY

Pace _____ Weather _____ Distance _____ Week total _____

SUMMARY

Week's total _____ Longest run _____ Shortest run _____

Average run _____ Month's total _____ Year's total _____

Daily Weight

	Wed _____
Sun _____	Thurs _____
Mon _____	Fri _____
Tues _____	Sat _____

Morning Pulse

	Wed _____
Sun _____	Thurs _____
Mon _____	Fri _____
Tues _____	Sat _____

WEEK OF _____

GOALS FOR WEEK _____

_____

In cold weather, don't overdress (dress in layers so one or more can be peeled away as you run; the hands and ears need the most protection, the legs the least), run at the warmest hour of the day if possible (noon or early afternoon), don't stop during a run or stand around outside afterwards for long enough to get chilled, and run with the wind behind you when you can.

SUNDAY

Pace_____ Weather _____ Distance _____ Week total_____

MONDAY

Pace_____ Weather _____ Distance _____ Week total_____

TUESDAY

Pace_____ Weather _____ Distance _____ Week total_____

WEDNESDAY

Pace_____ Weather _____ Distance _____ Week total_____

THURSDAY

Pace _____ Weather _____ Distance _____ Week total _____

FRIDAY

Pace _____ Weather _____ Distance _____ Week total _____

SATURDAY

Pace _____ Weather _____ Distance _____ Week total _____

SUMMARY

Week's total _____ Longest run _____ Shortest run _____

Average run _____ Month's total _____ Year's total _____

Daily Weight	Wed _____	**Morning Pulse**	Wed _____
Sun _____	Thurs _____	Sun _____	Thurs _____
Mon _____	Fri _____	Mon _____	Fri _____
Tues _____	Sat _____	Tues _____	Sat _____

WEEK OF _____

GOALS FOR WEEK _____

_____

Joggers are primarily interested in improving their physical fitness and doing so in a hurry. It's a perfectly legitimate and honorable ambition. Runners, however, become so wrapped up in the activity for other reasons—usually recreation, relaxation or competition—that fitness becomes little more than a by-product.

SUNDAY

Pace _____ Weather _____ Distance _____ Week total _____

MONDAY

Pace _____ Weather _____ Distance _____ Week total _____

TUESDAY

Pace _____ Weather _____ Distance _____ Week total _____

WEDNESDAY

Pace _____ Weather _____ Distance _____ Week total _____

THURSDAY

Pace _____ Weather _____ Distance _____ Week total _____

FRIDAY

Pace _____ Weather _____ Distance _____ Week total _____

SATURDAY

Pace _____ Weather _____ Distance _____ Week total _____

SUMMARY

Week's total _____ Longest run _____ Shortest run _____

Average run _____ Month's total _____ Year's total _____

Daily Weight Wed _____

Sun _____ Thurs _____

Mon _____ Fri _____

Tues _____ Sat _____

Morning Pulse Wed _____

Sun _____ Thurs _____

Mon _____ Fri _____

Tues _____ Sat _____

WEEK OF _____

GOALS FOR WEEK _____

_____

All degrees and descriptions of runners are alike in more ways than they're different. They all operate under the same physical laws. They all get more from running if they work within those laws, and they all suffer when they break them.

SUNDAY

Pace _____ Weather _____ Distance _____ Week total _____

MONDAY

Pace _____ Weather _____ Distance _____ Week total _____

TUESDAY

Pace _____ Weather _____ Distance _____ Week total _____

WEDNESDAY

Pace _____ Weather _____ Distance _____ Week total _____

THURSDAY

Pace _____ Weather _____ Distance _____ Week total _____

FRIDAY

Pace _____ Weather _____ Distance _____ Week total _____

SATURDAY

Pace _____ Weather _____ Distance _____ Week total _____

SUMMARY

Week's total _____ Longest run _____ Shortest run _____

Average run _____ Month's total _____ Year's total _____

Daily Weight

Wed _____

Sun _____ Thurs _____

Mon _____ Fri _____

Tues _____ Sat _____

Morning Pulse

Wed _____

Sun _____ Thurs _____

Mon _____ Fri _____

Tues _____ Sat _____

WEEK OF _____

GOALS FOR WEEK _____

_____

You pick what you plant. Just as you can't expect to put potatoes into the ground and harvest tomatoes, you can't become a runner by bowling or lifting weights.

SUNDAY

Pace _____ Weather _____ Distance _____ Week total _____

MONDAY

Pace _____ Weather _____ Distance _____ Week total _____

TUESDAY

Pace _____ Weather _____ Distance _____ Week total _____

WEDNESDAY

Pace _____ Weather _____ Distance _____ Week total _____

THURSDAY

Pace _____ Weather _____ Distance _____ Week total _____

FRIDAY

Pace _____ Weather _____ Distance _____ Week total _____

SATURDAY

Pace _____ Weather _____ Distance _____ Week total _____

SUMMARY

Week's total _____ Longest run _____ Shortest run _____

Average run _____ Month's total _____ Year's total _____

Daily Weight   Wed _____

Sun _____   Thurs _____

Mon _____   Fri _____

Tues _____   Sat _____

Morning Pulse   Wed _____

Sun _____   Thurs _____

Mon _____   Fri _____

Tues _____   Sat _____

WEEK OF _____

GOALS FOR WEEK _____

_____

Running is a stress. When it's applied in small doses, the body reacts by strengthening its defense against this and other stresses. Runners require specific and regular stresses in order to adapt and improve.

SUNDAY

Pace _____ Weather _____ Distance _____ Week total _____

MONDAY

Pace _____ Weather _____ Distance _____ Week total _____

TUESDAY

Pace _____ Weather _____ Distance _____ Week total _____

WEDNESDAY

Pace _____ Weather _____ Distance _____ Week total _____

THURSDAY

Pace _____ Weather _____ Distance _____ Week total _____

FRIDAY

Pace _____ Weather _____ Distance _____ Week total _____

SATURDAY

Pace _____ Weather _____ Distance _____ Week total _____

SUMMARY

Week's total _____ Longest run _____ Shortest run _____

Average run _____ Month's total _____ Year's total _____

Daily Weight

	Wed _____		
Sun _____	Thurs _____		
Mon _____	Fri _____		
Tues _____	Sat _____		

Morning Pulse

Wed _____	
Sun _____	Thurs _____
Mon _____	Fri _____
Tues _____	Sat _____

WEEK OF _____

GOALS FOR WEEK _____

_____

The running puzzle has two parts, and one is no good without the other. The two are work and rest. You can't go anywhere unless you work. But you can't work hard all the time. Rest must follow work as surely as a night's sleep follows a day's activity.

SUNDAY

Pace _____ Weather _____ Distance _____ Week total _____

MONDAY

Pace _____ Weather _____ Distance _____ Week total _____

TUESDAY

Pace _____ Weather _____ Distance _____ Week total _____

WEDNESDAY

Pace _____ Weather _____ Distance _____ Week total _____

THURSDAY

Pace _____ Weather _____ Distance _____ Week total _____

FRIDAY

Pace _____ Weather _____ Distance _____ Week total _____

SATURDAY

Pace _____ Weather _____ Distance _____ Week total _____

SUMMARY

Week's total _____ Longest run _____ Shortest run _____

Average run _____ Month's total _____ Year's total _____

Daily Weight

	Wed _____
Sun _____	Thurs _____
Mon _____	Fri _____
Tues _____	Sat _____

Morning Pulse

	Wed _____
Sun _____	Thurs _____
Mon _____	Fri _____
Tues _____	Sat _____

WEEK OF _____

GOALS FOR WEEK _____

_____

Run when you're eager, rest when you're tired, and learn to tell the two feelings apart. Knowing when to stop is as important as knowing how to start.

SUNDAY

Pace _____ Weather _____ Distance _____ Week total _____

MONDAY

Pace _____ Weather _____ Distance _____ Week total _____

TUESDAY

Pace _____ Weather _____ Distance _____ Week total _____

WEDNESDAY

Pace _____ Weather _____ Distance _____ Week total _____

THURSDAY

Pace _____ Weather _____ Distance _____ Week total _____

FRIDAY

Pace _____ Weather _____ Distance _____ Week total _____

SATURDAY

Pace _____ Weather _____ Distance _____ Week total _____

SUMMARY

Week's total _____ Longest run _____ Shortest run _____

Average run _____ Month's total _____ Year's total _____

Daily Weight

Wed _____

Sun _____   Thurs _____

Mon _____   Fri _____

Tues _____   Sat _____

Morning Pulse

Wed _____

Sun _____   Thurs _____

Mon _____   Fri _____

Tues _____   Sat _____

WEEK OF _____

GOALS FOR WEEK _____

_____

You can't run hard and fast until you can run easy and slow. Always be sure you can run a distance easily before you think about racing it.

SUNDAY

Pace _____ Weather _____ Distance _____ Week total _____

MONDAY

Pace _____ Weather _____ Distance _____ Week total _____

TUESDAY

Pace _____ Weather _____ Distance _____ Week total _____

WEDNESDAY

Pace _____ Weather _____ Distance _____ Week total _____

THURSDAY

Pace _____ Weather _____ Distance _____ Week total _____

FRIDAY

Pace _____ Weather _____ Distance _____ Week total _____

SATURDAY

Pace _____ Weather _____ Distance _____ Week total _____

SUMMARY

Week's total _____ Longest run _____ Shortest run _____

Average run_____ Month's total _____ Year's total _____

Daily Weight   Wed _____

Sun _____   Thurs _____

Mon _____   Fri _____

Tues _____   Sat _____

Morning Pulse   Wed _____

Sun _____   Thurs _____

Mon _____   Fri _____

Tues _____   Sat _____

S peed does no good unless it's built on top of a solid foundation of endurance. Yet it is true, too, that endurance can't be used in a race until speed training is added to it.

SUNDAY

Pace _____ Weather _____ Distance _____ Week total _____

MONDAY

Pace _____ Weather _____ Distance _____ Week total _____

TUESDAY

Pace _____ Weather _____ Distance _____ Week total _____

WEDNESDAY

Pace _____ Weather _____ Distance _____ Week total _____

THURSDAY

Pace _____ Weather _____ Distance _____ Week total _____

FRIDAY

Pace _____ Weather _____ Distance _____ Week total _____

SATURDAY

Pace _____ Weather _____ Distance _____ Week total _____

SUMMARY

Week's total _____ Longest run _____ Shortest run _____

Average run _____ Month's total _____ Year's total _____

Daily Weight

	Wed _____
Sun _____	Thurs _____
Mon _____	Fri _____
Tues _____	Sat _____

Morning Pulse

	Wed _____
Sun _____	Thurs _____
Mon _____	Fri _____
Tues _____	Sat _____

WEEK OF _____

GOALS FOR WEEK _____

_____

Try filling the wasted minutes with running. Get up a little earlier in the morning. Turn on the TV a little later in the evening. Substitute a run for lunch. Don't wait for running time to open up. Make time.

SUNDAY

Pace _____ Weather _____ Distance _____ Week total _____

MONDAY

Pace _____ Weather _____ Distance _____ Week total _____

TUESDAY

Pace _____ Weather _____ Distance _____ Week total _____

WEDNESDAY

Pace _____ Weather _____ Distance _____ Week total _____

THURSDAY

Pace _____ Weather _____ Distance _____ Week total _____

FRIDAY

Pace _____ Weather _____ Distance _____ Week total _____

SATURDAY

Pace _____ Weather _____ Distance _____ Week total _____

SUMMARY

Week's total _____ Longest run _____ Shortest run _____

Average run _____ Month's total _____ Year's total _____

Daily Weight

	Wed _____
Sun _____	Thurs _____
Mon _____	Fri _____
Tues _____	Sat _____

Morning Pulse

	Wed _____
Sun _____	Thurs _____
Mon _____	Fri _____
Tues _____	Sat _____

WEEK OF _____

GOALS FOR WEEK _____

_____

A running place is anyplace. Wherever you walk, you can run—parks, parking lots, bike paths, beaches, sidewalks, streets, schoolyards. Use whatever is available in your neighborhood. Choose quiet, pleasant-to-look-at routes over a variety of terrains and surfaces if you have a choice.

SUNDAY

Pace _____ Weather _____ Distance _____ Week total _____

MONDAY

Pace _____ Weather _____ Distance _____ Week total _____

TUESDAY

Pace _____ Weather _____ Distance _____ Week total _____

WEDNESDAY

Pace _____ Weather _____ Distance _____ Week total _____

THURSDAY

Pace _____ Weather _____ Distance _____ Week total _____

FRIDAY

Pace _____ Weather _____ Distance _____ Week total _____

SATURDAY

Pace _____ Weather _____ Distance _____ Week total _____

SUMMARY

Week's total _____ Longest run _____ Shortest run _____

Average run _____ Month's total _____ Year's total _____

Daily Weight	Wed _____	Morning Pulse	Wed _____
Sun _____	Thurs _____	Sun _____	Thurs _____
Mon _____	Fri _____	Mon _____	Fri _____
Tues _____	Sat _____	Tues _____	Sat _____

Nature takes away the explosiveness of youth and returns it to us as the persistence and staying power of maturity. Kids are natural sprinters. The rest of us are natural endurance athletes.

SUNDAY

Pace _____ Weather _____ Distance _____ Week total _____

MONDAY

Pace _____ Weather _____ Distance _____ Week total _____

TUESDAY

Pace _____ Weather _____ Distance _____ Week total _____

WEDNESDAY

Pace _____ Weather _____ Distance _____ Week total _____

THURSDAY

Pace _____ Weather _____ Distance _____ Week total _____

FRIDAY

Pace _____ Weather _____ Distance _____ Week total _____

SATURDAY

Pace _____ Weather _____ Distance _____ Week total _____

SUMMARY

Week's total _____ Longest run _____ Shortest run _____

Average run _____ Month's total _____ Year's total _____

Daily Weight

	Wed _____
Sun _____	Thurs _____
Mon _____	Fri _____
Tues _____	Sat _____

Morning Pulse

	Wed _____
Sun _____	Thurs _____
Mon _____	Fri _____
Tues _____	Sat _____

WEEK OF _____

GOALS FOR WEEK _____

_____

There will be bad days—perhaps more bad ones than good. But pushing through the bad ones will let you enjoy the good ones when they come. If you wait for perfect weather, you won't run very often.

SUNDAY

Pace _____ Weather _____ Distance _____ Week total _____

MONDAY

Pace _____ Weather _____ Distance _____ Week total _____

TUESDAY

Pace _____ Weather _____ Distance _____ Week total _____

WEDNESDAY

Pace _____ Weather _____ Distance _____ Week total _____

THURSDAY

Pace _____ Weather _____ Distance _____ Week total _____

FRIDAY

Pace _____ Weather _____ Distance _____ Week total _____

SATURDAY

Pace _____ Weather _____ Distance _____ Week total _____

SUMMARY

Week's total _____ Longest run _____ Shortest run _____

Average run _____ Month's total _____ Year's total _____

Daily Weight   Wed _____

Sun _____   Thurs _____

Mon _____   Fri _____

Tues _____   Sat _____

Morning Pulse   Wed _____

Sun _____   Thurs _____

Mon _____   Fri _____

Tues _____   Sat _____

WEEK OF _____

GOALS FOR WEEK _____

_____

Boredom is related to fatigue and to impatience. Run within your limits, allow more than enough time for running, think and look while on the run, and you shouldn't get bored.

SUNDAY

Pace _____ Weather _____ Distance _____ Week total _____

MONDAY

Pace _____ Weather _____ Distance _____ Week total _____

TUESDAY

Pace _____ Weather _____ Distance _____ Week total _____

WEDNESDAY

Pace _____ Weather _____ Distance _____ Week total _____

THURSDAY

Pace _____ Weather _____ Distance _____ Week total _____

FRIDAY

Pace _____ Weather _____ Distance _____ Week total _____

SATURDAY

Pace _____ Weather _____ Distance _____ Week total _____

SUMMARY

Week's total _____ Longest run _____ Shortest run _____

Average run _____ Month's total _____ Year's total _____

Daily Weight

	Wed _____
Sun _____	Thurs _____
Mon _____	Fri _____
Tues _____	Sat _____

Morning Pulse

	Wed _____
Sun _____	Thurs _____
Mon _____	Fri _____
Tues _____	Sat _____

WEEK OF _____

GOALS FOR WEEK _____

_____

Running isn't perfectly safe. But the precautions against trouble are so simple to take and the risks are so small that running should be considered no more dangerous than mowing the lawn.

SUNDAY

Pace _____ Weather _____ Distance _____ Week total _____

MONDAY

Pace _____ Weather _____ Distance _____ Week total _____

TUESDAY

Pace _____ Weather _____ Distance _____ Week total _____

WEDNESDAY

Pace _____ Weather _____ Distance _____ Week total _____

THURSDAY

Pace _____ Weather _____ Distance _____ Week total _____

FRIDAY

Pace _____ Weather _____ Distance _____ Week total _____

SATURDAY

Pace _____ Weather _____ Distance _____ Week total _____

SUMMARY

Week's total _____ Longest run _____ Shortest run _____

Average run _____ Month's total _____ Year's total _____

Daily Weight   Wed _____

Sun _____   Thurs _____

Mon _____   Fri _____

Tues _____   Sat _____

Morning Pulse   Wed _____

Sun _____   Thurs _____

Mon _____   Fri _____

Tues _____   Sat _____

Find your own line between enough and too much running, and stay just a little on the low side of it. That's the basic rule in all training. "The harder you work, the better you'll be" and "It has to hurt to do any good" are myths.

SUNDAY

Pace _____ Weather _____ Distance _____ Week total _____

MONDAY

Pace _____ Weather _____ Distance _____ Week total _____

TUESDAY

Pace _____ Weather _____ Distance _____ Week total _____

WEDNESDAY

Pace _____ Weather _____ Distance _____ Week total _____

THURSDAY

Pace _____ Weather _____ Distance _____ Week total _____

FRIDAY

Pace _____ Weather _____ Distance _____ Week total _____

SATURDAY

Pace _____ Weather _____ Distance _____ Week total _____

SUMMARY

Week's total _____ Longest run _____ Shortest run _____

Average run _____ Month's total _____ Year's total _____

Daily Weight

Wed _____

Sun _____   Thurs _____

Mon _____   Fri _____

Tues _____   Sat _____

Morning Pulse

Wed _____

Sun _____   Thurs _____

Mon _____   Fri _____

Tues _____   Sat _____

WEEK OF _____

GOALS FOR WEEK _____

_____

Plan to run with waves of effort. Not in a steady stream of same amount, same pace, same place every day, but by alternating harder runs and easier ones, long and short, work and recovery.

SUNDAY

Pace _____ Weather _____ Distance _____ Week total _____

MONDAY

Pace _____ Weather _____ Distance _____ Week total _____

TUESDAY

Pace _____ Weather _____ Distance _____ Week total _____

WEDNESDAY

Pace _____ Weather _____ Distance _____ Week total _____

THURSDAY

Pace _____ Weather _____ Distance _____ Week total _____

FRIDAY

Pace _____ Weather _____ Distance _____ Week total _____

SATURDAY

Pace _____ Weather _____ Distance _____ Week total _____

SUMMARY

Week's total _____ Longest run _____ Shortest run _____

Average run _____ Month's total _____ Year's total _____

Daily Weight   Wed _____

Sun _____   Thurs _____

Mon _____   Fri _____

Tues _____   Sat _____

Morning Pulse   Wed _____

Sun _____   Thurs _____

Mon _____   Fri _____

Tues _____   Sat _____

Racing Results

No.	Date	Site	Name	Distance	Type	Time/ Pace	Place/ Field

List all races (and time trials, if you wish). Tell how many races this makes for you; when, where, what it's
called; how long; type (road, track, etc.); time; pace per mile; placing and number of starters in the field.

Progress of Personal Records

Distance		
Time	Margin	Date

Distance		
Time	Margin	Date

Distance		
Time	Margin	Date

Distance		
Time	Margin	Date

Distance		
Time	Margin	Date

Distance		
Time	Margin	Date

Distance		
Time	Margin	Date

Distance		
Time	Margin	Date

Distance		
Time	Margin	Date

Distance		
Time	Margin	Date

Keep records for the most commonly run distances or courses. Update these lists each time you break a record by adding the new mark to the bottom. This shows your progress at a glance. "Margin" is the amount by which the record is improved.

Best Times, Year by Year

Distance		
Year	Age	Time

Distance		
Year	Age	Time

Distance		
Year	Age	Time

Distance		
Year	Age	Time

Distance		
Year	Age	Time

Distance		
Year	Age	Time

Distance		
Year	Age	Time

Distance		
Year	Age	Time

Distance		
Year	Age	Time

Distance		
Year	Age	Time

Keep records for the most commonly run distances. Record best marks for the year whether they are your all-time bests or not. "Age" is how old you are on the day of the run.

Training Records

Longest Single Run		
Amount	Margin	Date

Best Day's Total		
Amount	Margin	Date

Best Week's Total		
Amount	Margin	Date

Best Month's Total		
Amount	Margin	Date

Best Year's Total		
Amount	Margin	Date

Longest Streak		
Amount	Margin	Date

Other		
Amount	Margin	Date

Other		
Amount	Margin	Date

Update these lists each time you break a record by adding the new mark to the bottom. This shows progress of records at a glance. "Margin" is the amount by which the record is improved. A "Day's Total" may come in more than one run. A "Streak" is the number of days without missing a run.

Fitness Scorecard

1. Cardiovascular Health* _____
   0 under medical care for heart or circulatory problems
   1 such problems exist but medical care is not required
   2 past cardiovascular ailments have been pronounced "cured"
   3 no history of cardiovascular problems

2. Injuries** _____
   0 unable to do any strenuous work because of an injury
   1 level of activity is limited by the injury
   2 some pain during activity but performance isn't affected significantly
   3 no injuries

3. Illnesses** _____
   0 unable to do any strenuous work because of an illness
   1 level of activity is limited by the illness
   2 some during activity but performance isn't affected significantly
   3 no illnesses

4. First (or Most Recent) Run*** _____
   0 able to run less than a half-mile or five minutes without stopping
   1 ran between a half-mile and a mile (10–15 minutes) nonstop the first time
   2 completed between a mile and 1½ miles (10–15 minutes) the first time
   3 went more than 1½ miles or 15 continuous minutes

5. Running Background _____
   0 have never trained formally for running
   1 no running training within the last three years or more
   2 no running training within the last 1–2 years
   3 have trained for running within the last year

6. Other Related Activities _____
   0 not currently active in any regular sports or exercise programs
   1 regularly participate in "slow sports" such as golf, baseball, softball, football
   2 regularly practice vigorous "stop and go" sports such as tennis, basketball, soccer
   3 regularly participate in steady-paced, prolonged activities such as bicycling, hiking, swimming

7. Age   _____

   0 50s and older
   1 40s
   2 30s
   3 20s or younger

8. Weight   _____

   0 more than 25 pounds above your "ideal" weight
   1 16–25 pounds above your "ideal" weight
   2 6–15 pounds above your "ideal" weight
   3 within five pounds of "ideal" weight (or below ideal weight)

9. Resting Pulse Rate   _____

   0 80 beats per minute or higher
   1 in the 70s
   2 in the 60s
   3 in the 50s or below

10. Smoking   _____

   0 a regular smoker
   1 an occasional smoker
   2 have been a regular smoker but quit
   3 never have smoked regularly

Score yourself in each of the 10 areas and add up the total.

Total Score: _____

The test is reprinted from *Jog, Run, Race* by Joe Henderson (Mountain View, California: World Publications, 1977). A score of 20 or higher is excellent and indicates you probably can go directly into a running or racing program. A score of 10–19 is average for adults and shows enough fitness to enter a jogging program. If you score less than 10 points, you should forget about even jogging for now and concentrate on raising your score by walking.

Exceptions:

*If you have any history of heart or circulatory disease, participate only in closely supervised activities.

**If these injuries or illnesses are temporary, wait until they are cured before starting a jogging/running program (if they're chronic, adjust the program to fit your limitations).

***If you can run continuously for 1½ miles (15 minutes) or more, you are fitter than your score indicates.

Twelve-Minute Test

r. Kenneth Cooper devised this test of aerobic fitness. Try it at least once a year.

Men (distance in miles covered in 12 minutes)				
Fitness Category	**Age 29–less**	**Age 30–39**	**Age 40–49**	**Age 50–up**
Good	1.50–1.74	1.40–1.64	1.30–1.54	1.25–1.49
Excellent	1.75–up	1.65–up	1.55–up	1.50–up

Women (distance in miles covered in 12 minutes)				
Fitness Category	**Age 29–less**	**Age 30–39**	**Age 40–49**	**Age 50–up**
Good	1.35–1.64	1.25–1.54	1.15–1.44	1.05–1.34
Excellent	1.65–up	1.55–up	1.45–up	1.35–up

Your sex (men use top chart, women bottom)   _____

Your age (find appropriate column)   _____

Distance covered in 12 minutes   _____

Fitness rating (excellent, good or less)   _____

Excerpted from Jog, Run, Race, *by Joe Henderson. World Publications, Mountain View, California, 1977, p. 93.*

Schedule Planning

1. Decide on the total amount of time you plan to spend running each week or the total number of miles.   _____

2. What is your number of training days weekly?   _____

3. Figure the daily average needed to reach your quota (divide figure one by figure two).   _____

4. What is the projected length of the "short" runs? (divide figure three in half.)   _____

5. How long should the "long" runs be? (Multiply figure three by two.)   _____

6. Approximate "collapse point" (average daily distance or time multiplied by three).   _____

7. Weekly schedule (should include a long run and at least two short runs or rest days; others are near the average):
   Day One   _____
   Day Two   _____
   Day Three   _____
   Day Four   _____
   Day Five   _____
   Day Six   _____
   Day Seven   _____
   Total   _____

8. Make increases in time at the rate of about 10% per run per week (add three minutes to a 30-minute run, six minutes to an hour run, etc.; list the amounts to be added to your short, average and long runs).

Joe Henderson's Jog, Run, Race *includes this planning guide.*

Types of Courses

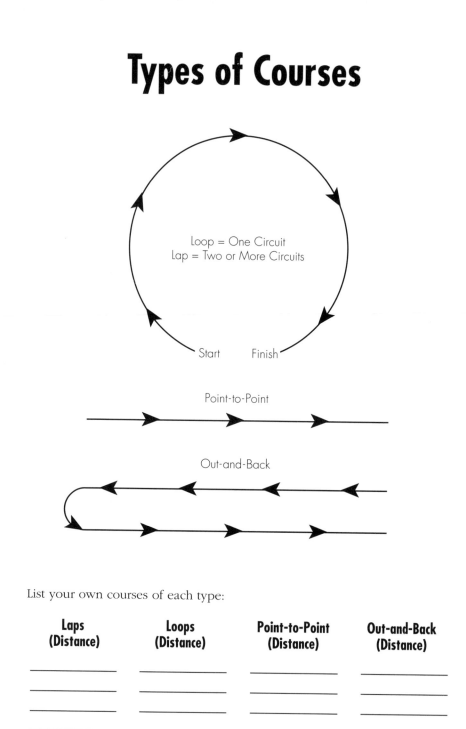

Loop = One Circuit
Lap = Two or More Circuits

Start   Finish

Point-to-Point

Out-and-Back

List your own courses of each type:

Laps (Distance)	Loops (Distance)	Point-to-Point (Distance)	Out-and-Back (Distance)

Excerpted from Jog, Run, Race, *by Joe Henderson. World Publications, Mountain View, California, 1977, p. 95.*

Distances and Metric Conversions

(Note: A kilometer is 1000 meters)

Meters	Yards/Miles
50	54 yards 6.5 inches
60	65 yards 1 foot 10.2 inches
100	109 yards 1 foot 1 inch
110	120 yards 10.7 inches
200	218 yards 2 feet 2 inches
300	328 yards 3 inches
400	437 yards 1 foot 4 inches
500	546 yards 2 feet 5 inches
600	656 yards 6 inches
800	874 yards 2 feet 8 inches
1000	1093 yards 1 foot 10 inches
1500	1640 yards 1 foot 3 inches
2000	1 mile 427 yards 8 inches
3000	1 mile 1520 yards 2 feet 6 inches
4000	2 miles 854 yards 1 foot 4 inches
5000	3 miles 188 yards 2.4 inches
6000	3 miles 1281 yards 2 feet
7000	4 miles 615 yards 10 inches
8000	4 miles 1708 yards 2 feet 8 inches
9000	5 miles 1042 yards 1 foot 6 inches
10,000	6 miles 376 yards 4.8 inches
12,000	7 miles 803 yards 1 foot
15,000	9 miles 564 yards 7.2 inches
20,000	12 miles 754 yards 9.6 inches
25,000	15 miles 940 yards 1 foot
30,000	18 miles 1128 yards 1 foot 2.4 inches
35,000	21 miles 1316 yards 1 foot 4.8 inches
40,000	24 miles 1504 yards 1 foot 7.2 inches
50,000	31 miles 120 yards 2 feet
60,000	37 miles 476 yards 2 feet 4.8 inches
70,000	43 miles 872 yards 2 feet 9.6 inches
80,000	49 miles 1249 yards 2.4 inches
90,000	55 miles 1625 yards 7.2 inches
100,000	62 miles 241 yards 1 foot

Yards/Miles	Meters
50 yards	45.72
60 yards	54.864
70 yards	64.008
100 yards	91.44
120 yards	109.728
220 yards	201.168
300 yards	274.32
330 yards	301.644
440 yards	402.336
500 yards	457.2
600 yards	548.64
660 yards	603.504
880 yards	804.672
1000 yards	914.4
1320 yards	1207.008
One mile	1609.344
2 miles	3218.688
3 miles	4828.032
4 miles	6437.376
5 miles	8046.72
6 miles	9656.064
7 miles	11,265.408
8 miles	12,874.752
9 miles	14,484.096
10 miles	16,093.44
15 miles	24,140.16
20 miles	32,186.88
Marathon	42,195
30 miles	48,280.32
40 miles	64,373.76
50 miles	80,467.2
60 miles	96,560.64
70 miles	112,654.08
80 miles	128,747.52
90 miles	144,840.96
100 miles	160,934.4

Most of the distances shown here, both English and metric, are standard racing events.

How Far Can You Go?

BASIC MILEAGE REQUIREMENTS

Weekly Total	Per Day	"Collapse"	Max. Race
10 miles	1½ miles	5 miles	3 miles
15 miles	2¼ miles	7 miles	5 miles
20 miles	3 miles	9 miles	6 miles
25 miles	3½ miles	11 miles	8 miles
30 miles	4¼ miles	13 miles	10 miles
35 miles	5 miles	15 miles	13 miles*
40 miles	5¾ miles	17 miles	15 miles
45 miles	6½ miles	20 miles	19 miles*
50 miles	7 miles	21 miles	19 miles*
55 miles	7¾ miles	23 miles	20 miles
60 miles	8½ miles	26 miles	20 miles
65 miles	9¼ miles	28 miles	Marathon
70 miles	10 miles	30 miles	Marathon
75 miles	10¾ miles	32 miles	31 miles*
80 miles	11½ miles	34½ miles	31 miles*
85 miles	12¼ miles	37 miles	31 miles*
90 miles	12¾ miles	39 miles	31 miles*
95 miles	13½ miles	41 miles	31 miles*
100 miles	14¼ miles	43 miles	31 miles*

"Collapse point" is approximately three times the daily average; maximum racing distance should be slightly below the collapse point.

* Twenty kilometers is slightly less than 13 miles, the half-marathon slightly more; 30 kilometers is just below 19 miles; 31 miles is about 50 kilometers.

Excerpted from Step Up to Racing. *World Publications, 1975, p. 24.*

How Often Should You Race?

These are Joe Henderson's recommended minimum recovery times from one race to the next, based on the amount of training and the racing distance.

AVERAGE RUNNING TIME PER DAY

	20 min.	30 min.	40 min.	50 min.	60 min.	70 min.
Mile	3 days	2 days	2 days	2 days	2 days	2 days
2 miles	5 days	4 days	3 days	2 days	2 days	2 days
3 miles	9 days	7 days	5 days	4 days	3 days	3 days
6 miles	20 days	14 days	10 days	8 days	7 days	6 days
10 miles		20 days	15 days	12 days	10 days	9 days
Half-Mar.			23 days	18 days	15 days	15 days
15 miles	not recommended		27 days	21 days	18 days	15 days
20 miles				30 days	25 days	21 days
Marathon					34 days	29 days

Minimum recovery time recommended from one race to the next—based on 10 times distance of race; allow at least 2 days for all.

Excerpted from Jog, Run, Race, *by Joe Henderson. World Publications, Mountain View, California, 1977, p. 196.*

Pacing Tables

PACING: ONE HOUR

Distance	Per Mile	Distance	Per Mile	Distance	Per Mile
7 miles	8:35.46	9 miles	6:40.00	11 miles	5:27.24
7¼ miles	8:16.50	9¼ miles	6:29.16	11¼ miles	5:20.00
7½ miles	8:00.00	9½ miles	6:19.02	11½ miles	5:13.08
7¾ miles	7.44.50	9¾ miles	6:09.24	11¾ miles	5:06.20
8 miles	7:30.00	10 miles	6:00.00	12 miles	5:00.00
8¼ miles	7:16.32	10¼ miles	5:51.24	12¼ miles	5:53.88
8½ miles	7:03.44	10½ miles	5:42.84	12½ miles	4:48.00
8¾ miles	6:51.42	10¾ miles	5:34.80	12¾ miles	4:42.36

PACING: 5–50 MILES

Mile	5 Miles	10 Miles	15 Miles	20 Miles	Marathon	50 Miles
5:40	28:20	56:40	1:25:00	1:53:20	2:28:34	
5:50	29:10	58:20	1:27:30	1:56:40	2:32:56	
6:00	30:00	1:00:00	1:30:00	2:00:00	2:37:19	5:00:00
6:10	30:50	1:01:40	1:32:30	2:03:20	2:41:41	5:08:20
6:20	31:40	1:03:20	1:35:00	2:06:40	2:46:03	5:16:40
6:30	32:30	1:05:00	1:37:30	2:10:00	2:50:25	5:25:00
6:40	33:20	1:06:40	1:40:00	2:13:20	2:54:47	5:33:20
6:50	34:10	1:08:20	1:42:30	2:16:40	2:59:09	5:41:40
7:00	35:00	1:10:00	1:45:00	2:20:00	3:03:33	5:50:00
7:10	35:50	1:11:40	1:47:30	2:23:20	3:07:55	5:58:20
7:20	36:40	1:13:20	1:50:00	2:26:40	3:12:17	6:06:40
7:30	37:30	1:15:00	1:52:30	2:30:00	3:16:39	6:15:00
7:40	38:20	1:16:40	1:55:00	2:33:20	3:21:01	6:23:20
7:50	39:10	1:18:20	1:57:30	2:36:40	3:25:23	6:31:40
8:00	40:00	1:20:00	2:00:00	2:40:00	3:29:45	6:40:00
8:10	40:50	1:21:40	2:02:30	2:43:20	3:34:07	6:48:20
8:20	41:40	1:23:20	2:05:00	2:46:40	3:38:29	6:56:40
8:30	42:30	1:25:00	2:07:30	2:50:00	3:42:51	7:05:00
8:40	43:20	1:26:40	2:10:00	2:53:20	3:47:13	7:13:20
8:50	44:10	1:28:20	2:12:30	2:56:40	3:51:35	7:21:40
9:00	45:00	1:30:00	2:15:00	3:00:00	3:56:00	7:30:00
9:10	45:50	1:31:40	2:17:30	3:03:20	4:00:22	7:38:20
9:20	46:40	1:33:20	2:20:00	3:06:40	4:04:44	7:46:40
9:30	47:30	1:35:00	2:22:30	3:10:00	4:09:06	7:55:00
9:40	48:20	1:36:40	2:25:00	3:13:20	4:13:28	8:03:20
9:50	49:10	1:38:20	2:27:30	3:16:40	4:17:50	8:11:40

PACING: 1–6 MILES

440	Mile	2 Miles	3 Miles	4 Miles	5 Miles	6 Miles
1:00	4:00					
1:01	4:04					
1:02	4:08	8:16				
1:03	4:12	8:24				
1:04	4:16	8:32	12:48	17:04		
1:05	4:20	8:40	13:00	17:20		
1:06	4:24	8:48	13:12	17:36	22:00	26:24
1:07	4:28	8:56	13:24	17:52	22:20	26:48
1:08	4:32	9:04	13:36	18:08	22:40	27:12
1:09	4:36	9:12	13:48	18:24	23:00	27:36
1:10	4:40	9:20	14:00	18:40	23:20	28:00
1:11	4:44	9:28	14:12	18:56	23:40	28:24
1:12	4:48	9:36	14:24	19:12	24:00	28:48
1:13	4:52	9:44	14:36	19:28	24:20	29:12
1:14	4:56	9:52	14:48	19:44	24:40	29:36
1:15	5:00	10:00	15:00	20:00	25:00	30:00
1:16	5:04	10:08	15:12	20:16	25:20	30:24
1:17	5:08	10:16	15:24	20:32	25:40	30:48
1:18	5:12	10:24	15:36	20:48	26:00	31:12
1:19	5:16	10:32	15:48	21:04	26:20	31:36
1:20	5:20	10:40	16:00	21:20	26:40	32:00
1:21	5:24	10:48	16:12	21:36	27:00	32:24
1:22	5:28	10:56	16:24	21:52	27:20	32:48
1:23	5:32	11:04	16:36	22:08	27:40	33:12
1:24	5:36	11:12	16:48	22:24	28:00	33:36
1:25	5:40	11:20	17:00	22:40	28:20	34:00
1:26	5:44	11:28	17:24	22:56	28:40	34:24
1:27	5:48	11:36	17:36	23:12	29:00	34:48
1:28	5:52	11:44	17:48	23:28	29:20	35:12
1:29	5:56	11:52	17:48	23:44	29:40	35:36
1:30	6:00	12:00	18:00	24:00	30:00	36:00
1:31	6:04	12:08	18:12	24:16	30:20	36:24
1:32	6:08	12:16	18:24	24:32	30:40	36:48
1:33	6:12	12:24	18:36	24:48	31:00	37:12
1:34	6:16	12:32	18:48	25:04	31:20	37:36
1:35	6:20	12:40	19:00	25:20	31:40	38:00
1:36	6:24	12:48	19:12	25:36	32:00	38:24
1:37	6:28	12:56	19:24	25:52	32:20	38:48
1:38	6:32	13:04	19:36	26:08	32:40	39:12
1:39	6:36	13:12	19:48	26:24	33:00	39:36

The left-hand columns show 440-yard and mile paces. If maintained exactly, they yield the times at right.

Heat Safety Index

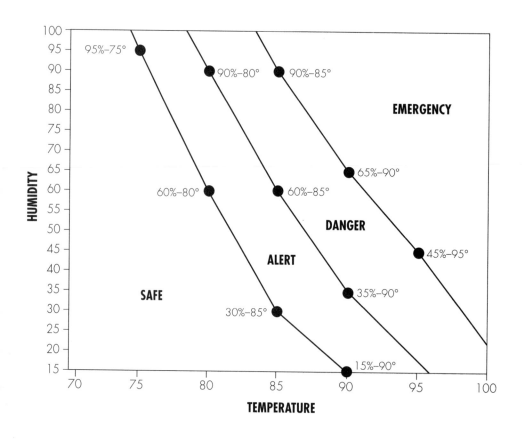

The chart is adapted from the Weather Service Operations Manual. "SAFE" temperature-humidity readings generally allow for normal activity. "ALERT" conditions require caution during long, hard runs. "DANGER" levels may demand a reduction of training. Strenuous running is not recommended during "EMERGENCY" conditions.

Wind-Chill Readings

Temperature (Fahrenheit)

Equivalent Chill Temperature

Wind	40	35	30	25	20	15	10	5	0	-5	-10	-15	-20	-25	-30	-35	-40	-45
Calm	40	35	30	25	20	15	10	5	0	-5	-10	-15	-20	-25	-30	-35	-40	-45
5	35	30	25	20	15	10	5	0	-5	-10	-15	-20	-25	-30	-35	-40	-45	-50
10	30	20	15	10	5	0	-10	-20	-25	-30	-35	-40	-45	-50	-60	-65	-70	-75
15	25	15	10	0	-5	-10	-20	-25	-30	-40	-45	-50	-60	-65	-70	-80	-85	-90
20	20	10	5	0	-10	-15	-25	-30	-35	-45	-50	-60	-65	-75	-80	-85	-95	-100
25	15	10	0	-5	-15	-20	-30	-35	-45	-50	-60	-65	-75	-80	-90	-95	-105	-110
30	10	5	0	-10	-20	-25	-30	-40	-50	-55	-65	-70	-80	-85	-95	-100	-105	-115
35	10	5	-5	-10	-20	-25	-35	-40	-50	-60	-65	-75	-80	-90	-100	-105	-115	-120
40*	10	0	-5	-15	-20	-30	-35	-45	-55	-60	-70	-75	-85	-95	-100	-110	-115	-125

Little Danger

Increasing Danger (Skin may freeze within one minute)

Great Danger (Skin may freeze within 30 seconds)

The wind makes temperatures feel colder than they look on the thermometer. The table lists the effects of wind force on the chill factor.

*Winds above 40 m.p.h. have little additional effect.

Ideal Weights

WOMEN

Height	Small Frame	Medium Frame	Large Frame
4'10"	92–98	96–107	104–119
4'11"	94–101	98–110	106–122
5'0"	96–104	101–113	109–125
5'1"	99–107	104–116	112–128
5'2"	102–110	107–119	115–131
5'3"	105–113	110–122	118–134
5'4"	108–116	113–126	121–138
5'5"	111–119	116–130	125–142
5'6"	114–123	120–135	129–146
5'7"	118–127	124–139	133–150
5'8"	122–131	128–143	137–154
5'9"	126–135	132–147	141–158
5'10"	130–140	136–151	145–163
5'11"	134–144	140–155	149–168
6'0"	138–148	144–159	153–173

MEN

Height	Small Frame	Medium Frame	Large Frame
5'2"	112–120	118–129	126–141
5'3"	115–123	121–133	129–144
5'4"	118–126	124–136	132–148
5'5"	121–129	127–139	135–152
5'6"	124–133	130–143	138–156
5'7"	128–137	134–147	142–161
5'8"	132–141	138–152	147–166
5'9"	136–145	142–156	151–170
5'10"	140–150	146–160	155–174
5'11"	144–154	150–165	159–179
6'0"	148–158	154–170	164–184
6'1"	152–162	158–175	168–189
6'2"	156–167	162–180	173–194
6'3"	160–171	167–185	178–199
6'4"	164–175	172–190	182–204

Caloric Cost of Running

CALORIES USED PER MILES OF RUNNING

Weight (Pounds)	Pace Per Mile								
	5:20	6:00	6:40	7:20	8:00	8:40	9:20	10:00	10:40
120	83	83	81	80	79	78	77	76	75
130	90	89	88	87	85	84	83	82	81
140	97	95	94	93	92	91	89	88	87
150	103	102	101	99	98	97	95	94	93
160	110	109	107	106	104	103	101	100	99
170	117	115	113	112	111	109	107	106	105
180	123	121	120	119	117	115	114	112	111
190	130	128	127	125	123	121	120	118	117
200	137	135	133	131	129	128	126	124	123
210	143	141	139	137	136	134	132	130	129
220	150	148	146	144	142	140	138	136	135

Note: Expenditure of 3500 calories equals one-pound weight loss.

CALORIES USED PER MINUTE

Weight (Pounds)	Pace Per Mile								
	5:20	6:00	6:40	7:20	8:00	8:40	9:20	10:00	10:40
120	15.6	13.8	12.1	10.9	9.9	9.0	8.3	7.6	7.0
130	16.9	14.8	13.2	11.8	10.7	9.7	8.9	8.2	7.6
140	18.1	15.9	14.1	12.6	11.5	10.5	9.6	8.8	8.1
150	19.4	17.0	15.1	13.5	12.3	11.2	10.2	9.4	8.7
160	20.6	18.1	16.1	14.5	13.0	11.8	10.9	10.0	9.3
170	21.9	19.2	17.0	15.3	13.8	12.7	11.5	10.6	9.8
180	23.1	20.2	18.0	16.2	14.6	13.3	12.2	11.2	10.4
190	24.4	21.3	19.0	17.0	15.4	14.0	12.9	11.8	10.9
200	25.6	22.4	19.9	17.9	16.2	14.8	13.5	12.4	11.5
210	26.9	23.6	20.9	18.7	17.0	15.5	14.1	13.0	12.1
220	28.1	24.7	21.9	19.6	17.8	16.2	14.8	13.6	12.6

Exercises

When I began running, stretching exercises were virtually unheard of. Day after day I did my warming up on the road. I left the house running, and generally quite hard.

I never thought much about warming up except for a track workout. And when I came back from a hard run I never thought much about warming down. My idea of warming up was a couple of seven-minute miles. And when I came back from a run I never stretched the tightness out of my body. I just headed straight for the shower.

I never had a stretching routine to loosen my body before a long run. I had never thought it necessary except prior to a fast track workout. The results of this were somewhat devastating. After a week of hard running, for instance, there were times when my hamstrings were so tight I could hardly keep my legs straight and touch my knees. Mercifully, that has all changed. Science and yoga have developed numerous stretching exercises to keep the body limber.

WHY STRETCH?

Weeks of running without stretching would tell you the reasons to use stretching exercises.

Running is an exercise that uses few muscles, and most of those are in the lower half of the body. When these muscles are used over and over in the repetition of running, they gradually become stiffer and stiffer. Frequently used muscles tend to tighten up. Over the course of running for a month without stretching, the normally limber person would find his muscles tightening like a piano string in a cold room. The result of this increasing tautness could be one of several possible injuries to muscles, tendons, and ligaments.

I was once asked by a novice if running can cause injuries that are fatal. Well, they aren't fatal to the individual, but they may be fatal to his or her running. The majority of running injuries occur from lack of proper stretching.

By not stretching, the body develops inflexibilities and strength imbalances in muscles and tendons. The result is an acute soreness that either slows you down or stops your running completely.

Inflexibility. One thing running doesn't do for you is increase flexibility. After all, running is an exercise in which the muscles are worked out by the repeated contractions which produce forward movement. After a muscle has been worked out it is likely to tighten up. Generally speaking, a tighter muscle is a shorter muscle.

As the muscles of your legs, calves, lower back, and buttocks tighten, they pull on each other at the connecting points. These muscles—just like a chain—are only as strong as their weakest points. Without proper stretching this weak area can be the site of a running injury. How can this inflexibility be overcome? The best way I know is stretching exercises. Stretching exercises now play an important role in my daily running. I do a series of stretches before each day's run, making sure the tendons and muscles that will have the toughest workout are stretched the most. But just stretching those muscles isn't enough. You have to take care of the other side—the side of your legs and torso that doesn't benefit directly from running.

Imbalance. The long-distance runner has a problem. Where middle-distance runners develop muscular balance from pushing and lifting their quadriceps, abdominals, hips, and groin muscles, the long-distance runner plods along, increasing the strength of his posterior muscles and tendons while relatively weakening the anterior muscles and tendons. As the lower back, hamstrings, buttocks, Achilles, and calves grow stronger through running, their counterparts stay the same or may even weaken.

Such imbalance can lead to the same sort of problems as inflexibility. The result of the inflexibility or imbalance is basically the same: it can make running so difficult that it takes you completely off you feet.

During my career I tried to run through injuries. This approach was on several occasions a severe mistake. Throughout my years of competition I had the misfortune to be injured so badly that I had to have surgery on nine different occasions. To say that not doing exercises shortened my competitive career is an understatement.

Proper running can be a joy. And stretching can keep it that way. The accompanying exercises are ones that I currently use to help keep me injury-free. Remember, improper stretching can be as bad as improper running.

FLEXIBILITY AND PREVENTIVE EXERCISES

Arm Swings. Stand with your arms straight out. Keeping them straight, rotate your arms in big circles both forward and backward. Concentrate on using your shoulders to do the work. This exercise will aid in shoulder flexibility. Repeat ten times for each arm.

Arm Swings

Thigh Stretch

Thigh Stretch. Grasping one foot behind you, try to pull your heel up to touch your buttocks. Do not arch your lower back. Do this for several seconds on each leg. This exercise will help thigh flexibility.

Groin Stretch. Stand with your feet together. Then, striding far out with one foot, lower yourself to the ground. Be careful not to do this too fast or to bounce when you reach your maximum stretch. Hold this position approximately ten seconds and stretch the other leg. What you want to feel are your groin muscles stretching. Do this exercise at least twice with each leg.

Groin Stretch

Calves Stretch

Calves Stretch. Stand about four or five feet from the wall, then lean against it with your hands. Keeping your feet flat against the floor, lower yourself against the wall. What you should feel are your Achilles tendons and calves being pulled. What you should *not* feel is any severe pain. Do this about eight times, holding each stretch for ten to fifteen seconds.

Trunk Twists. Stand comfortably with your hands on your hips and legs spread about shoulder width. Then turn in one direction, making sure not to move your feet. Repeat in the other direction. This exercise will loosen the lower back. Repeat this several times in both directions.

Side Bends. With your feet shoulder width apart, raise one arm above your head and leave the other at your side. Bend toward the arm that is down, feeling the pull down the side of your body. Repeat this action in the other direction. This exercise is good for trunk flexibility. Repeat several times.

Head Roll. In either a standing or sitting position, concentrate on relaxing your shoulders. Then slowly roll your head to the right a few times and then to the left. The purpose of this exercise is to add to neck flexibility and general relaxation. Repeat this exercise about ten times.

Hamstring Stretch. Sit on the floor, putting both legs together and straight out in front of you. Keeping your legs straight, reach out and grab your toes. If you can't reach your toes go for your ankles. Gradually and comfortably extend the stretch. What you should feel stretching are the muscles along the backs of your legs. Once again, beware of extreme pain. Do this six to eight times.

Hamstring Stretch

Backward Stretching

Backward Stretching. Lie flat on your back. Keeping your legs straight, bring them up over your head. Ideally your toes should be able to touch the floor behind your head. Many people, including me, can't reach the ideal. In that case just bring your feet over as far as possible, but do *not* force it! What you should feel stretching in this exercise are the muscles along the back of your legs and lower back. Do this three or four times.

Bent-Leg Sit-Ups

Bent-Leg Sit-Ups. Lay flat on your back. Put your hands behind your head, bend your knees to approximately a 45-degree angle and sit up. This motion will strengthen the abdominals and lower back. Repeat this motion several times. People with a back problem should only do a partial sit-up.

PREVENTIVE EXERCISES

Although ordinary stretching will help prevent many injuries, there are some areas of weakness that deserve special attention. For these areas I recommend preventive exercises.

Preventive exercises are used by many top athletes today to stop injuries before they start. Nature made some mistakes as far as the runner is concerned, but there is nothing the runner can do as far as changing nature. He must learn to live with these built-in handicaps. Preventive exercises are one of the ways to do this.

Lower Back Injury

A preventable running injury—and the one that has kept me out of running for more days than any other—is injury to the lower back. The most common would be irritation of the sciatic nerve that runs from the lower back and extends down the leg

Back injuries are often caused by an imbalance between the lower back muscles, which tighten and strengthen during running, and the abdominal muscles, which stay the same. The prevention for lower back problems and the ones I now use are the backward stretch and bent-leg sit-ups.

Sit-ups provide relief for the strained sciatic nerve as well as balancing strength between the abdominal and the back muscles. When the back muscles become stronger than the abdominal muscles, the sciatic nerve is stretched and irritated. By doing up to twenty-five sit-ups daily the runner can avoid lower back problems.

Backward stretches lengthen and stretch the muscles of the back that are tightened by running. However, care should be taken when doing this exercise because forcing it can result in injury to the upper back.

Knees

One of the larger slip-ups of nature is the knee joint. If you look at your leg it is not hard to understand what I mean. The knee is simply two long bones held together with a bit of muscle, cartilage, ligaments, and skin. Weak knees can play havoc with a runner and have been one of the major areas of injury for the running athlete.

Common knee injuries are chrondomalasia, or "runner's knee," and pain above the knee, which is usually an indication of a form of tendonitis.

How do you avoid these? One of the best ways is by doing leg lifts. Leg lifts were a major reason for my quick recovery from my two knee operations. As well as being beneficial in recovery they are very important in the prevention of knee injury.

Leg Lift. Performing a leg lift is quite simple. Get shoes, ankle weights, or even a paint can on the end of your foot. Sitting on the edge of a high bench from which your legs can dangle, slowly straighten your leg out in front of you and lower it back down again. Repeat this ten to fifteen times with each leg. Doing three to four sets of these with each leg every other night can help prevent common knee problems.

Leg Lift

Another running problem that requires special preventive exercises is shin splints. These are sores caused by a weakening of the shin muscles. The best way to head off shin splints is the shin strengthener.

Shin Strengthener. A good way to do this is to sit on a chair and, crossing one leg, push down on the toes as you pull up with your foot.

The result should be a flexing of the shin muscles. Repeat this fifteen to twenty times with each foot. Doing this exercise two to three times a week should keep your shins strong enough to prevent shin splints.

Although exercises won't totally eliminate the risk of injury from your running, they will certainly increase the number of hours you run injury-free. I look on exercises as being the preventive medicine of running. It is much easier to stop an injury before it develops than after.

Before an injury occurs, you should spend the few minutes a day it takes to do the exercises. After an injury happens, it can take days, weeks, and sometimes even months of recuperation to get back on the road.

If I had my competitive years to do over again, I would certainly devote far more time to thorough and effective stretching exercises. I think it would have saved me a lot of trouble.